Your Own
Joke Book

Compiled by **GERTRUDE CRAMPTON**

Cover by Erwin Hoffmann

Illustrations by Doug Andersen

SCHOLASTIC BOOK SERVICES

NEW YORK · TORONTO · LONDON · AUCKLAND · SYDNEY · TOKYO

16th printing . . . . November 1972

Printed in the U.S.A.

LITTLE WILLIES

Willie was quite a boy to have around the house.

Willie, at a passing gent
Threw a batch of fresh cement,
Crying, "Wait until you dry.
Then you'll be a real hard guy."

* * *

Willie saw some dynamite,
Couldn't understand it quite.
Curiosity never pays.
It rained Willie seven days.

* * *

Little Willie, home from school
Where he'd learned the Golden Rule,
Said, "If I eat all this cake,
Sis won't have a stomach-ache."

* * *

Little Willie on his bike
Through the village took a hike.
Mrs. Thompson blocked the walk.
She will live, but still can't talk.

Little Willie lit a rocket
Which his dad had in his pocket.
Next day he told Cousin Dan,
"Daddy is a traveling man."

* * *

Little Willie in the best of sashes
Fell in the fire and was burned to ashes.
By and by the room grew chilly,
But no one liked to poke up Willie.

* * *

Willie, hitting at a ball,
Lined one down the school-house hall.
Through his door came Dr. Hill.
Several teeth are missing still.

* * *

Little Willie from the mirror
Sucked the mercury off,
Thinking, in his childish error,
It would cure the whooping cough.
At the funeral his weeping mother
Smartly said to Mrs. Brown,
" 'Twas a chilly day for Willie
When the mercury went down."

HALF-CRACKED WISECRACKS

And don't you wish you'd cracked them?

A mother was teaching her small child the alphabet so that he'd be smarter than anybody when he started kindergarten. "Now," she said, "what comes after O?" "Yeah!" said the smart kid.

* * *

STUPID: "Hello, Jim. Fishing?"
DISGUSTED: "Nope. Drowning worms."

* * *

The doctor was very pleased with his patient's progress. "You're coughing more easily this morning."
Impatient patient: "Well, for gosh sakes, I ought to be. I've been practicing all night."

* * *

Smart Aleck took Stupid to the football game. Before the whistle blew, Smart Aleck said, "I can tell you the score of the game before it starts."
"Yeah?" said Stupid. "What?"
"Why," said Smart Aleck, "nothing to nothing."

HE: "Say, that's a bad gash you've got on your forehead. How in the world did you get it?"

HIM: "I bit myself."

HE: "Oh, come now. How could you bite yourself on your forehead?"

HIM: "I stood on a chair."

❋   ❋   ❋

"Good grief!" said the city slicker. "Why did they put the depot so far from the town?"

"I dunno," said the local yokel, "unless they wanted to get the depot just as close as possible to the railroad."

❋   ❋   ❋

PATIENT: "What shall I do? I have water on the knee."

TIRED DOCTOR: "Wear pumps."

❋   ❋   ❋

DOWNSTAIRS: "Didn't you hear me pounding on the ceiling?"

UPSTAIRS: "Oh, that's all right. We were making a lot of noise ourselves."

❋   ❋   ❋

SNOB: "Have any of your family connections ever been traced?"

SLOB: "Yes, they traced an uncle of mine as far as Canada once."

4

Proud: "All that I am I owe to my mother."

Loud: "Well, why don't you send her 30 cents and pay up the bill?"

* * *

A man made a mad dash through the station for the end of a train that was just pulling out. As he came back, the train caller said, "Just missed her, huh?"

"Oh, no," the tired man answered. "I was just chasing her out of the station."

YOUNG: "My father uses an umbrella he's had for twenty years."

YOUNGER: "For gosh sakes! He ought to return it."

* * *

The school was going to have a boxing team, and a lot of young fellows tried out for it. Some were good, and some were—not so good. One of the not-so-goods, after trying hard for a couple of rounds, said hopefully, "Have I done him any damage?"

"No," said the disgusted coach. "But keep on swinging. The draft may give him a cold."

* * *

The train came to a sudden stop, jerking the passengers around.

"What has happened, conductor?" cried one nervous old lady.

"Nothing much," said the conductor. "We hit a cow."

"Oh," said the relieved old lady. "Was it on the tracks?"

"No," replied the disgusted conductor. "We chased her into the barn."

* * *

FATHER: "When I was a boy, I thought nothing of a ten-mile walk."

SON, who is a little tired of hearing about the good old days: "Well, I don't think so much of it myself."

The visitor from the city stopped in at the village general store and asked, "Have you anything in the shape of automobile tires?"

"Yep," said the storekeeper. "Life preservers, doughnuts, and rubber bands."

* * *

MOTHER: "When that naughty boy threw stones at you, why didn't you come and tell me instead of throwing stones back at him?"

PRACTICAL KID: "What good would it do to tell you? You couldn't hit the side of a barn."

* * *

SUMMER BOARDER: "Does the water always come through the roof like this?"

FARMER: "No, sir. Only when it rains."

* * *

"Here, here, young man. You shouldn't hit that boy when he's down."

"G'wan. What do you think I got him down for?"

* * *

SMART: "More than 5,000 elephants go each year to make piano keys."

SMARTER: "Really? It's remarkable what animals can be trained to do."

Speeder: "Was I driving too fast?"
State Cop: "Heck, no! You were flying too low."

DRIVER'S LICENSE

*Don't let 'em tell any of these on you when you're ready
to drive Dad's car.*

Bill Muffet said
    His car couldn't skid.
This monument shows
    That it could and did.

— Newark, Ohio, *Advocate*

*   *   *

Oh, shed a tear
    For Luther Stover;
He tried to toot
    Two State cops over.

— New York *Sun*

*   *   *

FAMOUS LAST WORDS

Gimme a match. I think my gas tank's empty.
You can make it easy. That train isn't coming fast.
Step on her, boy. We're only doing seventy-five.
If you knew anything, you wouldn't be a traffic cop.

The rich man's daughter loved speed. Speed, speed, wonderful speed! Finally, when she got her driver's license, her father bought her a fine convertible which could reach a speed of 175 miles an hour.

The first morning she decided to have a little fun with the motorcycle cops. She went down the highway at 90, and a motorcycle cop gave chase. When he had almost, but not quite caught her, she raised her speed to 120. The cop opened the throttle. Again he almost caught her.

The girl decided to stop fooling around. So she jammed the accelerator right down to the floor. Away she went at 175 miles an hour. The cop disappeared in a cloud of dust.

Finally the girl turned around and went back to see why the cop wasn't chasing her. She found him wrecked in a ditch.

"I almost had you that last time," he said. "But you pulled away so fast that I thought my motorcycle had stopped. So I got off to see what had happened."

❋　❋　❋

"It says here in the newspaper," said the old gentleman, "that a man is run over in New York every half hour."

"Dear me!" said the old lady. "The poor fellow!"

❋　❋　❋

FLIBBERTY: "Arthur hasn't been out one night for three weeks."

GIBBET: "Has he turned over a new leaf?"

FLIBBERTY: "Nope. Turned over his dad's new car."

10

POLICEMAN: "You saw this lady driving toward you. Why didn't you give her half the road?"

UNHAPPY DRIVER: "I was going to, just as soon as I could find out which half she wanted."

* * *

Here lies the body of William Jay,
Who died maintaining his right of way.
He was right, dead right, as he sped along.
But he's just as dead as though he'd been dead wrong.

* * *

MOTHER: "What did your father say when you told him you'd smashed up the car?"
SON: "Shall I leave out the swear words?"
MOTHER: "Certainly."
SON: "He didn't say a word."

* * *

HE: "Does she know much about cars?"
HIM: "Naw. She thinks you cool the motor by stripping the gears."

* * *

GIRL FRIEND: "Henry! You mustn't drive so fast."
BOY FRIEND: "Why not?"
GIRL FRIEND: "The cop who's following us won't like it."

* * *

INTERESTED: "Have an accident?"
VICTIM: "No, thanks. I just had one."

11

"Now, class," said the teacher, "can you tell me one of the uses for cowhide?"

"Sure," said the Quiz Kid brightly. "It holds the cow together."

QUIZ KIDS

Oh, to be as smart as they are!

TEACHER: "Can you tell me anything about the great chemists of the seventeenth century?"

QUIZ KID: "They're all dead."

* * *

HISTORY TEACHER: "In what battle did General Wolfe, hearing of victory, cry, 'I die happy'?"

QUIZ KID: "His last battle."

* * *

TEACHER: "Give me, for any one year, the number of tons of coal shipped out of the United States."

QUIZ KID: "1492. None."

* * *

QUIZ KID: "By the way, did you know it is now the fashion to dress according to the color of your hair?"

QUIZ KIDDER: "No kidding!"

QUIZ KID: "Sure! A man with brown hair should wear a brown suit. A man with gray hair should wear a gray suit, and so on."

QUIZ KIDDER: "Say, tell me. How should a bald-headed man dress?"

* * *

TEACHER: "Where was the Declaration of Independence signed?"

QUIZ KID: "At the bottom."

Dad was leaving hurriedly to do an unexpected errand.

"By the way," he said, "if Mr. Jones comes in before I get back, tell him I'll meet him at the hotel at two o'clock."

"O.K.," agreed the Quiz Kid. "But what'll I tell him if he doesn't come?"

* * *

PASSENGER TO QUIZ KID: "Pardon me. Does this bus stop at Macomber Street?"

QUIZ KID: "Yep. Just watch me, and get off one stop before I do."

* * *

QUIZZ: "I don't know how to answer this question."

KID: "What's it say?"

QUIZZ: "It says, 'Who was your mother before she was married?' Heck, I didn't have any mother before she was married."

* * *

TEACHER, after a lesson about snow: "As we walk out on a cold winter day and look around what do we see on every hand?"

QUIZ KID: "Gloves."

* * *

SLIM: "For gosh sakes, Jim! I heard you were dead!"

JIM: "Yeah. They did say I was dead. But it was another fellow. I knew that it wasn't me as soon as I heard it."

A former Quiz Kid joined the Sea Scouts, and the head guy was quizzing him. "What would you do if a sudden storm sprang up on the starboard?"

"Throw out the anchor, sir," replied the former Quiz Kid.

"What would you do if another storm sprang up aft?" asked the head man.

"Throw out another anchor, sir," was the answer.

"And if another terrific storm sprang up forward, what would you do?"

"Throw out another anchor, sir."

"Hold on, there," said the head man. "Where are you getting all your anchors?"

"Oh," said the former Quiz Kid brightly, "from the same place you're getting all your storms."

If a Hottentot tot taught a Hottentot tot to talk e'er the tot could totter, ought the Hottentot tot be taught to say aught, or naught, or what ought to be taught her?

TWIZZLERS

If you can say these without making a mistake,
you're saying them too slowly.

A tutor who tooted the flute
Tried to teach two young tooters to toot;
　　Said the two to the tutor,
　　"Is it harder to toot, or
To tutor two tooters to toot?"

* * *

Had enough about Hottentots? If not, try this one—
If to hoot and to toot a Hottentot tot be taught by a
Hottentot tutor, should the tutor get hot if the Hottentot
tot hoot and toot at the Hottentot tutor?

* * *

A PUZZLING QUESTION

Does a doctor doctor a doctor according to the doctored doctor's doctrine of doctoring, or does the doctor doing the doctoring doctor the other doctor according to his own doctoring doctrine?

* * *

If a woodchuck could chuck wood, how much wood could a woodchuck chuck if a woodchuck could chuck wood? If a woodchuck could and would chuck wood, how much wood could a woodchuck chuck if a woodchuck would and could chuck wood?

Susan shineth shoes and socks. Shoes and socks shines Susan. She ceaseth shining shoes and socks for shoes and socks shock Susan.

* * *

SWAN IN THE SEA

We shouted, "Swim, Swan, swim!"
The swan swam and swam back again.
"What a swim, Swan, you swam!"

* * *

Theophilus Thistle, the thistle sifter, in sifting thousands of unsifted thistles, thrust thrice three thousand thistles through the thick of his thumb. Now, if Theophilus Thistle, the thistle sifter, in sifting thousands of unsifted thistles, thrust thrice three thousand thistles through the thick of his thumb, how many wouldst thou, in sifting thousands of thistles, thrust through the thick of thy thumb?

* * *

Knott and Shott fought a duel. Knott was shot, and Shott was not. It was better to be Shott than Knott.

* * *

Six brave maids sat on the bed braiding broad braids. Braid, brave maids!

* * *

She sells sea shells by the sea-shore.

Peter Piper picked a peck of pickled peppers. A peck of pickled peppers Peter Piper picked. If Peter Piper picked a peck of pickled peppers, where's the peck of pickled peppers Peter Piper picked?

* * *

A big black bug bit a big black bear. Where is the big black bear the big black bug bit?

He rocked the boat,
Did Ezra Shank.
These bubbles mark

Where Ezra sank.

FOR WRITING IN AUTOGRAPH BOOKS

Next time you need a "pome," try one of these.

Don't worry if your job is small
And your rewards are few.
Remember that the mighty oak
Was once a nut like you.

* * *

Mary had a little lamb,
A lobster and some prunes,
A glass of milk, a piece of pie,
And then some macaroons;
It made the naughty waiters grin
To see her order so,
And when they carried Mary out,
Her face was white as snow.

* * *

A doctor fell into a well
And broke his collar bone.
The doctor should attend the sick
And leave the well alone.

Ruth rode in my new car
In the seat beside me.
I took a bump at fifty-five
And rode on Ruthlessly.

* * *

You can always tell the English,
You can always tell the Dutch,
You can always tell the Yankees—
But you can't tell 'em much!

No word was spoken when they met,
By either—sad or gay,
And yet one badly smitten was,
As mentioned the next day.
They met by chance this summer eve,
With neither glance nor bow;
They often come together so—
A freight train and a cow.

* * *

She wore her stockings inside out
All through the summer heat.
She said it cooled her off to turn
The hose upon her feet.

* * *

Girls, girls, to me give heed—
In controlling men:
If at first you don't succeed,
Cry, cry again.

BOYS ONLY READ THIS

Out of two thousand four hundred and seventy-four
girls, there will be two thousand four hundred and sixty-
eight who will read this. The other six will be blind.

* * *

The night was growing old
As she trudged through snow and sleet.
Her nose was long and cold
And her shoes were full of feet.

Why didn't they play cards on Noah's ark?
Because Noah sat on the deck.

CONUNDRUMS

A conundrum is a stupid question that's so almighty stupid it needs a stupid answer. Like this:

CONUN: What is the animal that has the head of a cat, and the tail of a cat, and the ways of a cat, and yet isn't a cat?
DRUM: A kitten.

* * *

What animal would be likely to eat a relative?
An ant-eater.

* * *

Why should soldiers be rather tired on the first of April?
Because they've just had a march of thirty-one days.

* * *

Name the longest word in the English language.
Smiles. There's a mile between the first letter and the last one.

* * *

What is it that you cannot hold ten minutes, although it is as light as a feather?
Your breath.

There was a young man from the city
Who met what he thought was a kitty.
   He gave it a pat
   And said, "Nice little cat!"
They buried his clothes, out of pity.

LIMERICKS

Who ever heard of a joke book without limericks?

There was a young lady from Niger
Who smiled as she rode on a tiger.
　They came back from the ride
　With the lady inside
And the smile on the face of the tiger.

❋　❋　❋

There was a young lady of Lynn
Who was so excessively thin
　That when she essayed
　To drink lemonade
She slipped through the straw and fell in.

❋　❋　❋

"There's a train at 4:04," said Miss Jenny.
"Four tickets I'll take. Have you any?"
　Said the man at the door,
　"Not four for 4:04,
For four for 4:04 is too many."

❋　❋　❋

A canner, exceedingly canny,
One morning remarked to his granny,
　"One canner can can
　Anything that he can,
But a canner can't can a can, can he?"

There was a young woman named Bright
Whose speed was much faster than light.
   She set out one day,
   In a relative way,
And returned on the previous night.

A certain young fellow named Beebee
Wished to wed with a lady named Phoebe,
　　But he said, "I must see
　　What the minister's fee
Be before Phoebe be Phoebe Beebee."

❀　❀　❀

There was a young maid who said, "Why
Can't I look in my ear with my eye?
　　If I put my mind to it,
　　I'm sure I can do it.
You never can tell till you try."

❀　❀　❀

The bottle of perfume that Willie sent
Was highly displeasing to Millicent.
　　Her thanks were so cold
　　They quarreled, I am told,
Through that silly scent Willie sent Millicent.

❀　❀　❀

There was a young lady named Perkins
Who just simply doted on gherkins.
　　In spite of advice
　　She ate so much spice
That she pickled her internal workin's.

There was an old lady from Wooster
Who was often annoyed by a rooster.
   She cut off his head
   Until he was dead
And now he can't crow like he useter.

* * *

A cheerful old bear at the zoo
Could always find something to do.
   When it bored him, you know,
   To walk to and fro,
He changed it and walked fro and to.

* * *

There was a young fellow of Wheeling
Who had such delicate feeling
   When he read on the door,
   "Don't spit on the floor,"
He jumped up and spat on the ceiling.

* * *

A mouse in her room woke Miss Dowd,
She was frightened, it must be allowed.
   Soon a happy thought hit her.
   To scare off the critter,
She sat up in bed and meowed.

There was a young lady of Diss
Who said, "Now I think skating bliss!"
    Now no more will she state
    For a wheel off her skate
Made her finish up something like this.

❋   ❋   ❋

A boy and his girl friend, Min,
Skated out where the ice was quite thin.
    Had a quarrel, no doubt,
    For I hear they fell out.
What a blessing they didn't fall in!

❋   ❋   ❋

Watch this one. It's a toughie!

There was a man in Mich.
Who used to wish and wich.
    For spring to come
    So he could bum
And go away and fich.

❋   ❋   ❋

There once were two cats in Kilkenny
And each thought there was one cat too many;
So they quarreled and fit
And they gouged and they bit
Till, excepting their nails
And the tips of their tails,
Instead of two cats there weren't any.

The teacher had been giving a very long and not very interesting lecture on animals. When she finished, she decided to ask a few questions, and started off with this one: "Now, Tommy, tell me where elephants are found."

Tommy hadn't done much listening, but he was willing to do a little bluffing. "Elephants," said Tommy wisely, "are such darned big animals that they hardly ever get lost."

SCHOOL DAZE

*These may not help you get straight A's, but
they'll cheer you up if you don't.*

PROF: "Young man, are you the teacher of this class?"
YOUNG MAN: "No, sir."
PROF: "Then don't talk like an idiot."

❀ ❀ ❀

The Latin teacher was in fine humor after lunch and
instead of settling right down to Latin, he decided to tell
the class a couple of jokes he'd heard the night before.
Everybody laughed and laughed—except one girl in the
first row.

"What's the matter?" asked the Latin teacher. "Haven't
you got a sense of humor?"

"I don't have to laugh," said the girl. "I'm transferring
to another school Friday, anyhow."

❀ ❀ ❀

Mother was away, visiting her sister for a few days,
and Daddy got to wishing for a sponge cake.

"I'll make one," his daughter promised. "After all, I've
been taking home ec. for a month now."

Daddy agreed that would be swell. But when he got

home that night and asked for the sponge cake, daughter replied, "Well, I cooked it for you, but it didn't turn out right. I'll bet the grocer sent me the wrong kind of sponges."

* * *

CLASS PREZ: "Congratulate me! I won the election!"
POP: "Honestly?"
PREZ: "Oh, why bring that up?"

* * *

LAZY JOE: "Here's a certificate saying that I can't recite today."
DISGUSTED TEACHER: "Your doctor cheated you by making it just today."

* * *

The teacher was trying to get over to her class of young hopefuls the idea of addition. "Now," she said, "take the Smith family. There's the mother and the father and the baby. How many does that make?"
BRIGHT BOY: "Two, and one to carry."

* * *

ANNOYED FATHER: "Good heavens, son! Why aren't you at the top of your class once in a while, instead of always at the bottom?"
DUMB BUNNY: "It doesn't make any difference, Dad. The teacher talks so darned loud you can hear at both ends."

They were having a General Assembly for the whole school. The Student Council was running it, and doing a fine job. Some of the students told jokes (from this book, of course), a couple of girls tap-danced, and so on. Then four boys from the Student Council broke into song. "When Irish eyes are smiling—" they warbled.

Just then a woman began to sob softly, and the president of the Student Council noticed her. He tiptoed quietly down the aisle and whispered, "Gee, I didn't know you were Irish."

"I'm not," she sobbed. "I'm the new music teacher."

SCIENCE TEACHER: "What pine has the longest and sharpest needles?"

SMART JOE: "A porcupine."

* * *

MATHEMATICS TEACHER: "Now, if I lay three eggs here and five eggs over there, how many eggs will I have?"

INTERESTED PUPIL: "Well, to tell you the truth, I don't believe you can do it, sir."

* * *

The physics teacher was talking about displacement. "Miss Jones," he said, "would you be good enough to tell the class what happens when a body is placed in water?"

"Certainly," said Miss Jones, the most popular girl in the school. "The telephone rings."

* * *

DUMB: "I've added these numbers ten times."

TEACHER: "Good boy!"

DUMB: "And here are the ten answers."

* * *

FATHER: "Well, son, how are your marks?"

SON: "They're under water."

FATHER: "What do you mean, under water?"

SON: "Below C level."

STUDENT IN ART CLASS: "That, sir, is a cow grazing."
PUZZLED ART TEACHER: "Indeed? Where is the grass?"
STUDENT: "The cow has eaten it."
ART TEACHER: "But where is the cow?"
STUDENT: "You don't think she'd be silly enough to stay there after she'd eaten all the grass, do you?"

* * *

TEACHER OF CIVICS: "Who's the Speaker of the House?"
SMART KID: "Mother."

* * *

THE SAME CIVICS TEACHER: "Now, will anyone tell me of anything new of importance that has happened during the last twenty years?"
THE SAME SMART KID: "Me."

* * *

GEOGRAPHY LESSON

"Is she Hungary?" Jimmy asked Bill.

"Alaska," Bill replied.

"Yes, Siam," she said.

"All right. I'll Fiji," Bill promised.

"Oh, don't Russia self," Jimmy told Bill.

"Yeah, but what if she Wales?" Bill said.

"Give her a Canada Chile," Jimmy suggested.

"I'd rather have Turkey," she said.

So they had Turkey without any Greece.

When the waiter brought the check, Jimmy said, "Look and see how much Egypt you."

And the waiter threw them all out of the restaurant.

The school was having its opening dance and get-acquainted party in the gym. One of the boys had just finished dancing with a pretty new girl.

"Do you see that ugly sap standing over there?" he asked. "He's the new principal and the meanest guy I've ever seen."

"Is that so?" she demanded. "Do you know who I am?"

"Nope," said the boy.

"Well, I'm the principal's daughter."

"Yipe! Do you know who I am?" asked the boy.

"No," she said.

"Thank goodness!"

* * *

When they pulled the absent-minded professor, half drowned, from the lake, he sputtered, "How exasperating! I've just remembered that I can swim."

* * *

The clerk at the bookstore said to the student who was having a hard time in every subject, "Here's a book that'll do half your work for you."

"Swell," replied the eager student. "Give me two of 'em."

* * *

HEALTH LESSON

I sneezed a sneeze into the air;
It fell to the ground I know not where.
But hard and cold were the looks of those
In whose vicinity I had snoze.

"Did you give the principal my note?" asked the father.

"Yes, sir," his son answered. "But there isn't any use sending him any notes. He's blind as a bat."

"Blind? That's news to me," said the astonished father. "How do you know?"

"Sure he's blind," said the son. "Twice he asked me where my hat was, and there it was in plain sight on my head all the time."

❊ ❊ ❊

"Did you children ever see an elephant skin?" asked the teacher.

"I have," said the smart kid brightly.

"Where was it?" asked the teacher.

"On the elephant," said the smart kid, just as brightly.

❊ ❊ ❊

DAD, looking suspiciously at the dessert his daughter has whipped up: "What's this?"

DAUGHTER: "It's cottage pudding. We learned how to make it at school today."

DAD: "Well, I think I got a piece of shingle in my mouth."

❊ ❊ ❊

SOPHOMORE: "But I don't think I deserve quite a zero on this paper."

TEACHER: "Neither do I, but it's the lowest mark I can give."

The science teacher noticed that the class was getting tired. So to give everybody a chance to take it easy a while, he said, "If there are 50 states in the Union and a rocket ship could reach from here to the moon in fifty-nine minutes, how old am I?"

"Forty-four, sir," said one of the students.

"That's right," said the startled science teacher. "How did you know?"

"Oh," said the student, "my brother's twenty-two, and he's only half nuts."

* * *

Two old settlers got to talking about cooking.

"I got me one of them cookbooks once, but I couldn't never do a thing with it," said one.

"Too much fancy stuff, huh?" said one.

"You said it. Every dang one of them recipes began the same way: 'Take a clean dish . . .' That settled me right there."

* * *

"Are your mother and father in?" asked the teacher when the small boy opened the door.

"They was in," said the boy, "but they is out now."

"They was in! They is out!" exclaimed the teacher. "Where's your grammar?"

"Out in the kitchen making cookies."

* * *

English Literature Teacher: "If Shakespeare were here today, he would be looked on as a remarkable man."

Voice from the Back of the Room: "You aren't kiddin'. He'd be more than 300 years old."

SCIENCE TEACHER: "Can you explain radio for us, Arthur?"

ARTHUR: "Well, if you had a very long dog reaching from New York to Chicago, and you stepped on its tail in New York, it would bark in Chicago. That's telegraphy. Radio is exactly the same thing without the dog."

VERBS IS FUNNY

A boy who swims may say he swum,
But milk is skimmed and seldom skum,
And nails you trim; they are not trum.

When words you speak, these words are spoken,
But a nose is tweaked and can't be twoken,
And what you seek is seldom soken.

If we forget, then we've forgotten,
But things we wet are never wotten,
And houses let cannot be lotten.

The things one sells are always sold,
But fogs dispelled are not dispold,
And what you smell is never smold.

When young, a top you oft saw spun,
But did you see a grin ever grun,
Or a potato neatly skun?

✹ ✹ ✹

PROF: "Name two pronouns."
STUDE: "Who, me?"

SNOBS AND SNORES

A sure cure for boredom.

BORE: "Speaking of Africa makes me think of the time—"

BORED: "Good heavens, you're quite right. I had no idea it was so late. Good-by."

* * *

ONE: "You say Bill is pretty cocky and sure of himself?"

THE OTHER: "I'll say he is. He does crossword puzzles with a pen."

* * *

"How do you like your hair cut?" asked the barber. And the tired teacher replied, "Off."

* * *

SHE: "Why do you call your boy friend a small-talk expert?"

HER: "If there's nothing to say, he'll say it."

* * *

On a rainy day a beautifully dressed snob in a mink coat got on a bus.

"Heavens," she said as she paid her quarter, "I don't suppose I've been in a bus for two years. I always take my own car."

The bus driver shifted gears and looked her over sourly. "Lady," he said, "you don't know how we've missed you."

The Willoughbys, who lived in Chicago, had a new housekeeper. She wasn't very bright, but she was a splendid cook. So the Willoughbys didn't care whether she was smart or not.

One night at dinner time the telephone rang, and the new housekeeper hurried to answer. She listened and laughed and said, "It certainly is!" and hung up.

A few seconds later the phone rang again. The new housekeeper answered it, listened, laughed, said, "It certainly is!" and hung up again.

"For goodness sake," bellowed Mr. Willoughby. "What's going on?"

"Silliest darned thing," answered the new housekeeper. "Some joker keeps calling up just to say, 'It's long distance from New York.'"

* * *

Sap: "Say, have you got ten million dollars?"
Slap Happy: "Well, not in cash."

* * *

"Oh, yes," said the snobbish young lady, "my family can trace its ancestors back to William the Conqueror."

"Next thing you'll be telling us that your ancestors were in the Ark with Noah," sniffed her friend.

"Gracious, no!" said the snobbish young lady. "My people had a boat of their own."

44

"What happened at the dance you crashed?" demanded the junior.

"I got thrown out the back door on my face," admitted the other junior. "So I told the usher I belonged to one of the most important families in town."

"So what happened then?"

"So he begged my pardon, asked me in again, and threw me out the front door."

* * *

SHE: "All extremely bright men are conceited."
HE: "Oh, come now. That isn't true. I'm not."

* * *

SNOB: "My ancestors came over on the *Mayflower*."
SLOB: "It's lucky for them. Immigration laws are stricter now."

* * *

The father of one of the football players was a well-known doctor. One day he dropped in to watch a scrimmage game. The coach pointed out the players and then said, "My best man is on the bench, because he's limping badly. He sprained his ankle at our last game. What would you do, doctor, in his case?"

"I'd limp, too," decided the doctor.

* * *

BORE: "I passed your house yesterday."
BORED: "Thanks awfully."

"That new member of Student Council seems to have a pretty good opinion of himself," said the president.

"You're not fooling," agreed the secretary. "On his last birthday he sent his mother a letter of congratulations."

* * *

It was one of these big, formal affairs everybody has to go to at least once in his life. The Smiths had to go and they insisted upon taking their house guest with them. The guest didn't see why he should be punished. So after a few minutes he said to the man next to him, "Gee, this thing is a bore. I'm going to beat it."

"I would too," said the other man, "But I've got to stay. I'm giving the party."

* * *

"I must be going," said the bore at last.

"Don't let me keep you if you really must be going," said the bored hostess.

"Yes, I must really go. But I did enjoy our visit. Do you know when I came in here, I had a headache? But now I've lost it completely."

"Oh, it isn't completely lost," said the hostess. "I've got it now."

There wasn't anything that John Henry Jones couldn't and wouldn't talk about. He took every conversation by the throat and choked it to death.

Finally Adam Smith couldn't stand any more.

"Do you realize," said Adam one day, "that you and I know all there is to be known?"

"Do you think so?" said John Henry, very pleased, for, after all, Adam was president of his class. "How do you figure that?"

"Easy," said Adam. "You know everything except that you are a darned idiot. And I know that."

* * *

Conceited football player, after a long and boring talk about how wonderful he was sure he was: "But enough about me, old man. Let's talk about you. Tell me — how do you think I played that last game?"

* * *

A very successful man had worked very hard all his life to become the success that he was.

It happened one day that he was invited to a party given by a very snobbish woman. During the evening his hostess told him how sorry she was to learn that he had been born in a small coal-mining town.

"What a shame!" cried the hostess. "Why in the world did you have to be born there?"

The successful man gave her a cold look and replied, "Oh, I just wanted to be close to my mother."

FROSH: "I woke up last night with the feeling that my watch was gone. So I got up and looked for it."

SOPH: "Was it gone?"

FROSH: "Nope, but it was going."

FOR THE SCHOOL PAPER

Does your school paper have jokes as good as these?

MODERN HIAWATHA

He killed the noble Mudjokivins.
Of the skin he made him mittens,
Made them with the fur side inside,
Made them with the skin side outside.
He, to get the warm side inside,
Put the inside skin side outside,
Put the warm side fur side inside.
That's why he put the fur side inside,
Why he put the skin side outside,
Why he turned them inside outside.

Excuse us, Mr. Longfellow.

* * *

"Glad to see you getting to school on time these mornings," said the teacher.

"Yes, sir, I've got a parrot now."

"A parrot, young man! I told you to get an alarm clock."

"I never seem to hear alarm clocks," explained the student. "But now I've got this parrot. And what the parrot says when the alarm wakes him up is enough to wake up anybody."

The more we study, the more we know.
The more we know, the more we forget.
The more we forget, the less we know.
The less we know, the less we forget.
The less we forget, the more we know.

WHY STUDY?

* * *

HE: "What's the difference between a sigh, a car, and a donkey?"

SHE: "I give up."

HE: "Well, a sigh is 'Oh, dear!' A car is too dear."

SHE: "And what's a donkey?"

HE: "You, dear."

* * *

TEACHER: "Why don't you like our school, James?"

JAMES: "Oh, it's not the school. It's the principal of the thing."

(Before you use this one, you better be sure your principal has a sense of humor.)

* * *

I often pause and wonder
At fate's peculiar ways.
For nearly all our famous men
Were born on holidays.

* * *

DRIP: "Can you stand on your head?"

DROP: "Nope. It's too high."

I said, "This horse, sir, will you shoe?"
And soon the horse was shod.
I said, "This deed, sir, will you do?"
And soon the deed was dod.

I said, "This stick, will you break?"
At once the stick he broke.
I said, "This coat, sir, will you make?"
And soon the coat he moke.

* * *

STOOP: "That's a queer pair of socks you have on —
one red and the other green."
STUPID: "Yeah. And the funny thing about it is that
I've got another pair at home exactly like this one."

* * *

DUMB: "Do you want to get next to something there's
a lot of money in?"
DUMBER: "Sure."
DUMB: "Well, go downtown and lean up against the
bank."

* * *

BORE: "I heard something this morning that opened
my eyes."
BORED: "Me, too — the alarm clock."

DRUGGIST: "That Wilson boy who used to work after school for you wants me to give him a job. Is he steady?"

GROCER: "Steady? If he was any steadier, he'd be motionless."

* * *

The freshman had to take care of his little brother and keep him quiet outdoors while Mother tried to get over her headache. Suddenly Mother was disturbed by loud roars from Little Brother.

"Willie," Mother called from the bedroom, "what's your little brother crying for? Didn't I tell you to give him anything he wanted?"

"Yes," agreed the freshman. "But now that I've dug him the hole he wanted, he wants me to bring it into the house."

* * *

"Dick," said his mother, "I wish you would run across the street and see how old Mrs. Rush is."

"Yes'm," said Dick.

He bounced back in a few minutes and said, "Mrs. Rush says it's none of your darned business how old she is."

* * *

"Is this a healthful place?" the new student asked the president of the Student Council.

"It sure is," said the Prez. "When I came here, I couldn't say a word. I had hardly a hair on my head.

I hadn't the strength to walk across the room, and I had to be lifted from my bed."

"My, you certainly look healthy now," said the new student. "How long have you been here?"

"Oh, I was born here."

* * *

WAITRESS: "Tea or coffee?"
CUSTOMER: "Coffee, please. Without cream."
WAITRESS: "You'll have to take it without milk. We haven't any cream."

* * *

CAPTAIN: "What did that seasick teacher say when you asked him if you could bring him anything?"
STEWARD: "He said, 'Bring me an island.'"

* * *

SLOW: "When I see you, I always think of Bud Jones."
SLOWER: "But I'm not a bit like Bud Jones."
SLOW: "Oh, yes, you are, You both owe me two bits."

* * *

Who was the smallest man in history?
That sailor who went to sleep on his watch, of course.

* * *

PUPIL: "After rain falls, when does it get up again?"
OUR SCIENCE TEACHER: "In dew time, my boy, in dew time."

HALF: "So you're going to start a bakery?"
BAKED: "Yep. If I can raise the dough."

❈ ❈ ❈

TABLOID BIOGRAPHY

High chair
High school
High stool
High finance
High hat
"Hi, Warden!"

❈ ❈ ❈

WHISPER: "Her dad cleaned up a fortune in crooked dough."

HUSH: "No kiddin'. What was he, anway, a counterfeiter?"

WHISPER: "Nope, a pretzel manufacturer."

❈ ❈ ❈

QUIZZ: "What's the difference between a lemon and a head of cabbage?"

WHIZZ: "I don't know."

QUIZZ: "Boy, you'd be a swell one to send after lemons!"

❈ ❈ ❈

LEFTY: "That means fight where I come from."
HEFTY: "Well, why don't you fight?"
LEFTY: "Because I ain't where I come from."

Adam and Eve were naming the animals of the earth, when along came a rhinoceros.

Adam said, "What shall we call this one?"

"Let's call it a rhinoceros," suggested Eve.

"Why?" asked Adam.

"Well," said Eve, "it looks more like a rhinoceros than anything else we've seen."

*　*　*

A little boy stood in the entrance of the shoe repair man's shop, watching the man at work.

"Say, mister," the little boy said at last, "what do you repair shoes with?"

"Hide," said the repair man.

"What?" said the little boy in surprise.

"I said hide," repeated the shoe man.

"What for?" demanded the boy.

"Hide! Hide! The cow's outside," explained the man.

"I don't care if it is," said the little boy. "Who the heck's afraid of a cow?"

*　*　*

LADY, shopping in a pet store: "I like this dog, but his legs are too short."

CLERK: "Too short! Why, all four of 'em reach the floor!"

*　*　*

SHE: "I was out of town when the class play was given. Did it have a happy ending?"

HER: "Sure. Everybody was glad it ended."

A couple of the fellows decided to be big he-men and went camping in the woods. Nine thousand mosquitoes were there too. At last our two brave men pulled the blankets over their heads to keep the mosquitoes away.

Finally one peeked out to see if the mosquitoes had left, and happened to see a few lightning bugs.

"It's no use," he told the other pioneer. "We might as well give up and go home. The darned mosquitoes are out looking for us with lanterns now."

GRANDMOTHER: "You can catch more flies with molasses than you can with vinegar."

PRACTICAL GRANDDAUGHTER: "Sure, but what do I want with a flock of flies?"

*　*　*

There was going to be a big school doing, and Junior needed some extra cash. So he put a little heat on Dad, but Dad wouldn't melt.

"I'll tell you, though," said Dad. "The druggist needs help. Why don't you go down and see him? Maybe he'll give you a part-time job. You could be his right-hand man."

"Shucks!" said Junior in great disappointment. "I'm left-handed."

*　*　*

"The school's on fire!" shouted a passing motorist to the sophomore one Saturday morning.

"I know it," nodded the sophomore.

"Then why aren't you doing something about it?" cried the motorist.

"Oh, I am! I am!" replied the sophomore. "Ever since it started, I've been hoping for rain."

*　*　*

SMITH, reading facts and figures from his dad's insurance tables: "Do you know that every time I breathe, a man dies?"

JONES: "Why don't you use a little mouth wash now and then?"

DEAR EDITOR: Why do they use knots instead of miles on the ocean?

ANSWER: Because they've got to keep the ocean tide.

* * *

"Was it hot here in August?" asked the young thing who'd spent her vacation in the mountains.

"Hot?" said the had-to-stay-home. "Say, I saw a hound dog chasing a rabbit one day, and they were both walking."

* * *

A farmer once called his cow "Zephyr"
She seemed such an amiable hephyr.
   When the farmer drew near,
   She kicked off his ear,
Which made him considerably dephyr.

* * *

BOY FRIEND: "Have a peanut?"

GIRL FRIEND: "No, thanks. They're fattening."

BOY FRIEND: "Aw g'wan. Why should they be fattening?"

GIRL FRIEND: "I don't know why, but I never saw an elephant eating anything else."

* * *

DEAR EDITOR: What's worse than raining cats and dogs?

ANSWER: Hailing streetcars and buses.

BIG MUSCLES

Some people think they're so big and
brawny that it's fun to take them
down a peg or two.

PRINCIPAL: "How's Smitty on the high jump? Any good?"

COACH: "Naw. He can hardly clear his own throat."

* * *

BRAIN: "I can beat you in a race any day, if you let me choose the course and if you give me just a yard head start."

TWINKLE LEGS: "O.K., you're on. What's the course?"

BRAIN: "Up a ladder."

* * *

The coach was putting the class through a course of exercises to toughen them up, and one fellow with more brain than muscle began to get tired.

"Every man on his back!" barked the coach. "Legs up in the air! Now pretend that you're riding a bicycle. Faster! Faster!"

The tired one waved his legs a few times, and then stopped.

"Hey you!" shouted the coach. "What's the idea?"

"Who, me?" said the bright one. "I'm just coasting down a hill."

Bill got special permission to go deer hunting with his dad, and he was pretty excited about it. One day he hurried back to camp, and on the way he met the guide.

"John," he said to the guide, "are all the fellows out of the woods yet?"

"Yep," said John.

"Dad and all the rest of them?"

"Yep Your father and all the rest of them," said the guide.

"You're sure?" asked Bill.

"Sure I'm sure," said John.

"And they're all safe?"

"Every one of them," said the guide.

"Oh boy!" said Bill. "Then I've shot a deer."

＊　＊　＊

GIRL, arriving at the end of the third inning: "What's the score, Harry?"

HARRY: "Nothing to nothing."

GIRL: "Goody, goody! We haven't missed a thing."

＊　＊　＊

GAL: "Is he really as fast a runner as they say he is?"

HAL: "Fast? He can run so fast that all the fellows he races with have to run twice as fast as he does just to keep up with him."

FIRST HUNTER: "I just met a great big bear back there in the woods."

EXCITED FRIEND: "Good! Did you give him both barrels?"

FIRST HUNTER: "The heck with both barrels. I gave him the whole darned gun."

❈　❈　❈

A fisherman was having a wonderful time in a trout stream. Of course, the fishing season hadn't opened and he hadn't any license, but he was having a wonderful time anyhow. Finally a stranger walked up.

"Any luck?" asked the stranger.

"Any luck! Boy, oh boy! This is a wonderful spot. I took forty out of this stream yesterday."

"Is that so? By the way," the stranger said, "do you know who I am?"

"Nope."

"Well, meet the game warden," said the stranger.

"Oh," gulped the fisherman. "Well, do you know who I am?"

"Nope."

"Well, meet the biggest liar in the state."

* * *

A football player, wanting to keep in good condition, got a job for the summer on a farm. He worked in the fields from dawn until dark, day after day, and he had to finish his chores by lantern light.

At the end of the first month he went to the farmer and said, "I'm going to quit. You promised me a steady job of work."

"Well, haven't you got a steady job of work?" asked the farmer in surprise.

"Nope," said the football player. "There are three or fours hours every night when I don't have anything to do except fool away my time sleeping."

* * *

SOPH: "Where's Jim this afternoon?"

FROSH: "If he knows as much about canoes as he thinks he does, he's out canoeing. But if he doesn't know any more about canoes than I think he does, he's out swimming."

The coach thought soccer might be a good game to use to get his football squad into better condition. So he got everybody together — scrubs and stars alike — and explained how to play soccer.

"Now, remember, fellows," he finished, "if you can't kick the ball, kick a fellow on the other team. Now let's get busy."

The coach looked about. "Where the dickens is that soccer ball?"

One of the scrubs shouted, "To heck with the ball. Let's start the game!"

❋ ❋ ❋

DUMB: "I don't see how football players ever get clean."

DUMBER: "Silly! What do you think the scrub team is for?"

❋ ❋ ❋

JUNIOR: "Dad, what happens to a ball player when his eyesight begins to fail?"

DAD: "They make an umpire out of him."

❋ ❋ ❋

The school was blessed with a fine back on the team. He was a cinch to be named on the All-State team. But the football coach was very anxious to keep him from getting big-headed and so whenever he had a chance, the coach would pull him down a peg.

One day the back picked up a fumble on his own ten-yard line and tore down the field for the winning touchdown.

In the locker room the coach tried to hang on to his own excited joy. After all, the back mustn't get conceited.

"You started too slow," he told the back. "You should have gone down the other side of the field. There were fewer men to take out on that side. And I didn't care at all for the way you stiff-armed the safety man. I think you should have side-stepped him."

The back thought it all over, and then said, "Well, Coach, how was it for distance?"

＊　＊　＊

During an exciting game of football, one of the players had a couple of fingers badly smashed. The team doctor rushed him off the field and examined and dressed his hand.

"Doctor," asked the player anxiously, "when my hand heals, will I be able to play the piano?"

"Certainly you will," promised the doctor.

"You're a wonderful doctor," said the happy football player. "I never could play the piano before."

＊　＊　＊

SHE: "Did you get hurt when you were on the football team?"

HE: "Nope. It was while the team was on me."

＊　＊　＊

HE: "Look! Our captain is going to kick a goal."
SHE: "He is? What did the goal do?"

New President of New Boxing Club: "Now there is the question of colors for our club. Are there any suggestions?"

New Member: "How about black and blue?"

* * *

"How would you like to learn to ski?"

"Oh, I'd jump at the chance."

* * *

The coach put up a notice for the first football practice of the season, and one of the fellows who turned out was so fast on his feet that he made the other runners look like so many turtles. The coach called him over to the bench and asked him how he had learned to run so fast.

"We used to live in Texas," explained the boy, "and I used to catch jack rabbits on my father's ranch."

"That's an oldie," smiled the coach. "A lot of fellows here say the same thing, but they're not so fast as you."

"Well, my dad was pretty fussy about the rabbits he ate," the boy continued. "I not only had to chase 'em. I had to run alongside of them and feel them to see if they were fat enough for Dad before I caught 'em."

BABY-SITTER: "Why did you put this frog in your little sister's bed?"

PROBLEM: "Because I couldn't find a mouse."

JOKES FOR BABY-SITTERS

*If you're a baby-sitter, or know a baby-sitter,
read these and pass 'em along. They may
make baby-sitting easier for baby.*

BABY-SITTER: "Here, here! You mustn't pull the kitty's tail."

SONNY: "Don't yell at me. Yell at the cat. I'm only holding. The cat's doing the pulling."

* * *

The baby-sitter was trying to make the time pass pleasantly for the young hopeful by asking about the animals in his picture book.

They got to the picture of zebras, and the baby-sitter said, "What do zebras have that no other animals have?"

And the smart young hopeful replied, "Little zebras."

* * *

Mother was getting ready to go out, leaving the baby-sitter in charge.

"Now, Patrick, you behave yourself while Daddy and I are gone," she warned.

Patrick replied, "I'll be good for a nickel, Mummy."

Mummy: "Why don't you be more like your daddy? I don't have to give him a nickel to be good."

Patrick: "Oh, who wants to be like Daddy? He's good for nothing."

He was a brat. And he'd been more of a brat than usual. The baby-sitter was trying to get the little darling to sleep before she went entirely out of her little pink mind.

"Won't go to sleep," said the little darling. "Won't, won't, until you tell me a story. Please, please, please, please!"

"All right," said the worn-out baby-sitter. "Once there was a little girl named Little Red Riding Hood and she met a wolf and the wolf ate up her grandmother. Now go to sleep."

* * *

Little Benny's mother went shopping, and the baby-sitter was to stay with Benny all afternoon and get his supper for him.

Benny went out for a stroll, and when the baby-sitter called him in for an early meal, Benny said importantly, "I've just seen a man who makes horses."

"You have?" said the startled baby-sitter. "Are you sure?"

"Yep," said Benny. "He had the horse nearly finished when I saw him. He was just nailing on the back feet."

And who could be mean enough to tell Benny he'd seen a blacksmith shoeing a horse? Not the baby-sitter.

* * *

The baby-sitter had two charges that night. The four-year-old was contented with his picture book, but the baby was practically knocking the walls down with her yelling.

"Did the angels send baby down from heaven?" asked the four-year-old at last.

"Yes," said the frantic baby-sitter.

And the four-year-old summed it up nicely when he said, "They like to have it nice and quiet up there, don't they?"

*　*　*

ROSEMARY: "I wouldn't want you to say anything to my folks about it, but I don't think they know very much about bringing up children."

BABY-SITTER: "Where'd you get that idea?"

ROSEMARY: "Well, they make me go to bed when I'm wide awake, and they make me get up when I'm awfully sleepy."

*　*　*

WILLIE: "Mama says we're here to help others."

BABY-SITTER: "Of course we are."

WILLIE: "Well, what are the others here for?"

*　*　*

"Bobby! Bobbeeee! Where are you?" called the baby-sitter. "I've been calling you for the last twenty minutes."

Receiving no answer, she began to search — through the living room, the bedroom, the attic, the back porch.

"Bobby!" she called, as she went to the front porch. And there was real anger in her voice. "Bobby! Are you out there?"

"Well, no," came Bobby's voice. "Have you tried the cellar yet?"

Johnny was quite a boy. Daddy felt a bit sorry for the sitter who was to look after him. So before leaving for the theater, Daddy said, "Johnny, if you're good every minute of the time Mother and I are gone, I'll give you a dime when I get home."

After a long, hard evening, Daddy and Mother came home.

"Well, how about it, Johnny?" said Daddy. "I'm going to leave it up to you. Do you deserve the dime?"

Johnny looked at the baby-sitter.

Finally he muttered, "I owe you four bits."

* * *

The baby-sitter was pushing the baby carriage along a path in the park when a policeman strolled up.

"Fine-looking baby," he said. "How old is he?"

"He'll be a year old next week," answered the baby-sitter.

"He doesn't look that old," said the policeman.

"No," replied the baby-sitter. "You see, he was very young when he was born."

* * *

The baby-sitter was embarrassed to death. Just as she'd got hold of Jimmy and was dragging him home after a fight, they met the minister. The minister took one horrified look at Jimmy's black-eye.

"My boy," he said, "I pray you will never fight again and that you may never receive another black eye."

"That's O.K.," said Jimmy. "You better go home and pray about your own kid. I gave him two of 'em."

* * *

SMALL DAUGHTER: "Why is Daddy singing so much tonight?"

MOTHER: "He's trying to sing the baby to sleep before the baby-sitter gets here."

SMALL DAUGHTER, thoughtfully: "You know, if I was the baby, I'd pretend I was asleep."

* * *

SITTER: "What are you running for, Howie?"

HOWIE: "I'm trying to keep two fellers from fighting."

SITTER: "Goodness! What two fellows?"

HOWIE: "Sid Smith and me."

* * *

The small girl the baby-sitter was taking care of had fallen down and skinned her knees quite badly. So the small girl was weeping bitterly.

"I wouldn't cry like that if I were you," said the baby-sitter.

"You can cry any way you like," said the small girl. "This is the way I cry."

JUNIOR: "Sister and I are going to play elephants at the zoo while Mother and Daddy are gone. You can play, too."

BABY-SITTER: "What on earth can I do?"

JUNIOR: "You can be the lady who gives the elephants peanuts and candy."

* * *

The sitter was meeting for the first time the little boy she was to take care of.

"Do you go to school?" she asked.

"Naw," said the little tough. "I'm sent."

* * *

Any baby-sitter can tell you that
this is a true story:

"It is amazing that Mrs. Brown can never see any faults in her children," said Mrs. Smith.

"Mothers never can," laughed Mr. Smith.

"What a silly thing to say! Just like a man! I'm sure I could see faults in our children — if they had any."

* * *

The kindergartener amused himself while his folks were gone by sitting at his mother's desk and scratching a pencil along a sheet of his mother's notepaper.

"Writing a letter to your mother?" asked the baby-sitter.

"Nope, writing a letter to myself."

"Well," smiled the baby-sitter, "that's nice. What are you going to write to yourself?"

"How should I know? I haven't got the letter yet."

SMART COMEBACKS

And don't you wish you'd said 'em?

SLIP: "I always drink lots of milk, because my doctor says milk is a great bone-builder."

SHOD: "Looks to me as though your drinks are going to your head."

* * *

HIM: "I'd like to see something cheap in a loafer jacket."

CLERK: "Try this one, and the mirror's right behind you."

* * *

BORED: "You're really a very pretty girl."

SILLY: "Now, now! You'd say so even if you didn't think so."

BORED: "Sure. And you'd think so even if I didn't say so."

* * *

PEGGY: "She says she can date anybody she pleases."

LEGGY: "Too bad she doesn't please anybody."

* * *

Ali Baba went up to the entrance of the cave and cried, "Open, Sesame!"

And a voice from the cave replied, "Sez who?"

WIT: "Ugh! What's worse than finding a worm when you bite into an apple?"

HALF WIT: "Finding half a worm."

* * *

NOSEY: "I see you have your arm in a sling. Broken?"

NICE: "Yes, sir."

NOSEY: "Accident?"

NICE: "No. I tried to pat myself on the back."

NOSEY: "What for?"

NICE: "For minding my own business."

* * *

SHE: "Do you know her to speak to?"

HER: "No. Only to talk about."

* * *

BILL: "You dance very well."

BETTY: "I wish I could say the same about you."

BILL: "Oh, you could if you were as big a fibber as I am."

* * *

"Is a chicken big enough to eat when it's two weeks old?" asked the farmer's son.

"Of course not," said the teacher.

"Then how does it manage to live?"

KIT: "Have you noticed Jane's new bathing suit?"
KAT: "No, I haven't. What does it look like?"
KIT: "In most places it's a lot like Jane."

＊　＊　＊

SMART: "Did you hear the story about the peacock?"
ALECK: "Nope."
SMART: "It's a beautiful tale."

＊　＊　＊

SHE: "I'm not myself tonight."
HE: "Then we ought to have a good time."

＊　＊　＊

He was showing off in a restaurant. "Waiter," he ordered, "we want chicken — the younger the better." "Yes, sir," replied the tired waiter. "Eggs."

＊　＊　＊

"Is the dance formal, or can I wear my own clothes?"

＊　＊　＊

FIRE CAPTAIN: "What's the only piece of fire apparatus that won't go up a one-way street?"
ROOKIE: "A fireboat."

＊　＊　＊

"She took up horseback riding to reduce. So far she's taken off twenty-three pounds — off the horse."

75

A fresh guy crashed a private dance. When he was leaving, he still had enough nerve to walk up to the hostess and say, "Thanks for a lovely evening."

"Oh, that's all right," said the hostess. "Remind me to invite you the next time."

❋ ❋ ❋

JUDGE: "Have you ever been up before me?"
PRISONER: "I dunno. What time do you get up?"

❋ ❋ ❋

FROSH: "I always do my hardest work before breakfast."
FROSHER: "What's that?"
FROSH: "Getting up."

❋ ❋ ❋

PILOT: "Wanna fly?"
THRILLED: "Oh, boy! Sure!"
PILOT: "Wait a minute. I'll catch one for you."

❋ ❋ ❋

NERVE: "Lend me half a buck."
MEEK: "I've only got forty cents."
NERVE: "O.K. Lend me the forty cents. You can owe me a dime."

❋ ❋ ❋

"I know I'm right," stormed the sophomore. "And I'd rather be right than be president."

"Don't worry," said the senior. "You'll never be either."

TALL TALES

Can you top these?

A hunter was telling about his trip into the wilds, and said, "I got into the middle of a field and met the biggest bear I ever saw in my life. He was at least twelve feet tall, and his paws were a full twelve inches wide.

"There was only one tree in the field, and I ran for my life for that tree. It was a very old and very tall tree, and the first branch was a good twenty-five feet from the ground."

"Goodness!" cried one of the listeners. "What did you do?"

"What could I do?" demanded the hunter. "The bear was right behind me, his hot breath on my neck. So I jumped for that branch."

"Did you make it?" asked his listeners.

"Well, no," said the hunter, "not going up. But I caught it coming down."

* * *

A group of old fellows at the hotel got to talking about horses, especially race horses. Finally one old man spoke up.

"Horses!" he said. "You can't tell me anything about horses. I owned the fastest horse in this state once.

"Just to give you a rough idea about how fast that horse could run, let me tell you about a storm we were in. I was out about fifty miles from home that day, and a terrible storm came up. I turned the horse's head for home. And do you know, he raced that storm so close for the last twenty miles that I didn't feel a drop of rain, while my dog, who was only ten feet behind me, had to swim the whole way!"

* * *

Two men decided to fight a duel with pistols. One of the men was very, very fat, and when he noticed how thin the other man was, he got pretty excited.

"I'm twice as big a target as he is!" shouted the fat man. "I ought to stand twice as far away from him as he stands from me."

The thin man agreed, but somehow they couldn't work it out. So at last the fat man's second said, "Take it easy. I'll fix this."

Taking a piece of chalk from his pocket, he drew two lines down the fat man's coat, leaving a space between them.

"Now," he said to the thin man, "fire away. But, remember, any hits outside the chalk lines don't count."

If you think they've got some foolish rules where you live, take a look at some of these:

California's law says that it is a misdemeanor to shoot at any kind of game bird or mammal — except a whale — from an automobile or airplane.

In Kansas — "When two trains approach each other at a crossing, they shall both come to a full stop, and neither shall start up until the other has gone." No foolin'.

A Nebraska town once passed a law making it illegal for a barber to eat onions between seven in the morning and seven at night.

And in Alabama "any person who engages in domino playing on Sunday must be fined."

A town in West Virginia says, "No lions shall be allowed to run wild on the streets of this city."

*　*　*

Speaking of bears and hunters, an old hunter was spinning a tall tale about the time he was chased by a bear, and his grandchildren were listening hard.

"That bear came on and on and on," said Grandpa, "and I could feel his hot breath on the back of my neck. So I turned around when I was tired of running and I says to him, 'Mr. Bear, you have met your master.'"

"What did you do, Grandpa?" the children asked.

"There wasn't anything to it at all," said Grandpa. "I just put my hand into that old bear's mouth and reached in as far as I could and grabbed him by the tail. Then I pulled hard. Well, sir, that doggone bear turned inside out and ran the other way."

VISITOR FROM THE CITY: "Does the corn grow pretty good here in Kansas?"

KANSAS FARMER: "Pretty good! Say, last year a boy wanted to see how the sky looked, and the corn was so high and so thick that he couldn't see anything above him except corn. So he climbed a corn stalk to take a look around, and that stalk grew so fast that the boy couldn't climb down as fast as the stalk took him up. Finally the boy was clear out of sight. Three men took the job of cutting down the stalk, but the stalk grew so fast that they couldn't hit it twice in the same place with their axes.

"The boy lived on green corn and threw down about four bushels of cobs. He might have frozen to death from being pushed up so high if he hadn't been rescued by a helicopter the Navy sent over."

* * *

"It was so cold where we were," bragged the explorer, "that the candles froze and we couldn't blow them out."

"That's nothing," said his pal. "Where we were, the words came out of our mouths in pieces of ice, and we had to fry them to find out what we were talking about."

* * *

"Speaking of good soil," said the farmer, "I never saw a place where melons grow like they used to grow up my way. The first year I planted them, I thought my fortune was made. But I didn't harvest a one of them."

"Why was that?" asked his cousin from the city. "I thought you said the soil was good."

"Too good," said the farmer. "The vines grew so fast

in that good soil that they wore out the melons dragging
'em around."

* * *

A farmer and his wife went to the County Fair, and
the farmer was very interested in the airplanes flying
about. So he got to talking with one of the pilots.

"Why don't you take a ride?" asked the pilot.

"How much?" asked the farmer.

The pilot told the farmer that the charge for a ten-
minute ride was ten dollars.

"Ten dollars!" said the farmer. "Why, that's a dollar
a minute. I couldn't enjoy the trip if I had to pay that
much. Isn't there any way you could let us ride for less
money?"

The pilot liked to play a joke once in a while; so he
said, "Well, I'll tell you what I'll do. I'll take you and
your wife up for nothing if you'll promise not to say a
word all the time we're in the air. But one yip out of
either of you and it's going to cost you the full ten dollars. Is that O.K.?"

"That's O.K.," said the farmer.

So the farmer and his wife got into the plane, which
was an open job. A few minutes later they were soaring
over the countryside.

When the pilot had gained enough altitude, he began
to try to make the farmer yell. He looped and whip-
stalled and rolled — did every trick he knew. But the
farmer and his wife remained silent.

At last the pilot gave up and returned to the ground.

"Well," he said when they'd landed, "I want to congratulate you. You've won, and the ride's free. You're a

brave man. Not many men could go through what you did on the very first trip and not yell."

The farmer smiled proudly and replied, "Well, I guess so. But I can tell you, you almost caught me there once — when my wife fell out."

*　*　*

The old gentlemen were sitting around in the club, telling one story after another. But the new member hadn't opened his mouth.

"Come, now, sir," said one of the old-timers. "Surely something interesting has happened in your life. Tell us about it."

"Well," said the new member, "I did have an interesting experience once. I was in a shipwreck."

So the new member described the shipwreck very excitingly, and the old members were impressed. The new member had reached the point in his story where only he and the captain and a half dozen others were left on the sinking ship, after the last of the lifeboats had been lowered.

"And then," he said, "a great wave came — so huge that it shut out the sky. It crashed down upon the sinking ship, and under its terrible force the ship sank. All those left on board were drowned."

The new member stopped, and the old members thought about this exciting story. But at last one of them said, "And you — what became of you?"

"Me?" said the new member. "Oh, I drowned right along with the rest of them."

TRAMPS AND SCAMPS

*What would you say if an old tramp came to
your door and asked for a piece of pie?
Here are some ideas.*

The old tramp knocked on the back door and asked
for a hand-out.

"Did you see that big pile of wood?" asked the farm
wife.

"Yeah, I seen it," said the tramp.

"Such grammar!" said the farm wife. "You should say
you saw it."

"Lady," grinned the tramp, "you saw me see it, but
you ain't seen me saw it."

* * *

Two tramps were stretched out lazily on the green
banks of a quiet river. The sun was warm, and the river
was cool and still. Above them the birds sang cheerfully.

"Gosh," said one tramp happily, "right now I wouldn't
trade places with a guy who had a million dollars."

"How about five million?" asked his pal.

"Not even for five million," yawned the tramp.

"Well," said his pal, "how about ten million?"

The tramp sat up.

"That's different," he said. "Now you're talking real
dough."

HOUSEWIFE: "You should be ashamed to be seen begging at my house."

TRAMP: "Oh, don't feel like that. I've seen worse houses than this one."

*   *   *

The tramp got the usual question along with the hand-out.

"How did you happen to become a tramp?" asked the lady of the house.

"Doctor's orders, ma'am," answered the tramp.

"Oh, come, now," said the lady of the house. "I can't believe that."

"It's the truth," said the tramp. "He told me to take long walks after meals."

*   *   *

FARMER'S WIFE: "Out of work, are you? Well, there's a pile of wood that needs splitting, and I was just going to send for a man to split it."

HOBO, anxious to help: "Is that so? Where does he live? I'd be glad to get him for you."

*   *   *

TRAMP: "Say, mister, can you give me two dollars for a cup of coffee?"

MISTER: "Two dollars? A cup of coffee is never more than a dime."

TRAMP: "Oh, I know it. But I'm putting all my begs in one ask-it."

"I'm a self-made man," said the snobbish tramp. "I started life without a rag on my back, and now I'm covered with rags."

A tramp knocked at the back door of a farm house.

"Lady," he said sadly, "would you help a poor man out of his troubles?"

"Certainly," said the hot and tired woman. "Would you rather be shot or hit with an ax?"

* * *

INTERESTED LADY: "You'd have more chance of getting a job if you shaved, and cleaned your clothes neatly, and had your hair cut."

HOBO: "I know it, lady, I know it. I found that out years ago."

* * *

Tramp, piece of pie in his hand, said to the housewife: "If it's all right with you, lady, I'd rather saw the pie and eat the wood."

* * *

"Good gracious!" said Mrs. Hawley. "Why don't you get a job?"

"Oh, I would," said the tramp. "But everybody wants references from the last fellow I worked for."

"Well, why don't you get them?" asked Mrs. Hawley.

"Why, bless your heart, lady," smiled the tramp. "The last fellow I worked for has been dead for twenty years."

* * *

TRAMP: "What's worrying you, old pal?"

TEARFUL HOBO: "I found a wonderful recipe for homemade pie, and I ain't got no home."

"You did me a favor ten years ago," said the old tramp, "and I never forgot it."

"Oh," replied the good man, very pleased with himself, "and you have come back after all these years to repay me?"

"Well, no," said the tramp. "I just got into town and need another favor. So I thought of you right away."

* * *

"These old trousers may be useful to you," said the kind old lady. "All they need is a little mending."

"That's fine," said the tramp. "I'll call back for them in half an hour."

* * *

An old fellow, out of work, took to tramping the roads. At noon, he got up enough courage to knock on Mrs. Wheeler's back door to ask for a bite to eat.

Mrs. Wheeler, hot and tired from doing the washing, threw open the door and snapped, "Did you wish to see me?"

The old fellow backed away quickly.

"Well, if I did, ma'am, I got my wish, thank you."

* * *

"Can you oblige me with something to eat?" asked the hobo.

"Certainly," said the lady. "Go out to the woodshed and take a few chops."

Why Don't They Teach the Cow to Do It?

Help wanted: Man for fruit-tree spraying, also to take charge of cow who can sing in the choir and blow organ.

— Anniston (Cal.) *Gazette*

NOTES IN THE NEWS

The newspapers don't always get it right.

What a Cow!
C. H. has bought a cow, and he is now supplying his neighbors with milk, butter, and eggs.

— Vermont *Newspaper*

✻　✻　✻

What Happened to the Bride?
After a wedding reception at Sherry's, the bridegroom left on a honeymoon.

— Boston *Post*

✻　✻　✻

Oh, I Don't Know, Some People Are Smart
Visit our clothing department. We can outwit the whole family.

— Advertisement in Bayonne (N.J.) *Daily News*

✻　✻　✻

Don't Be So Critical
The bride was gowned in white lace. The bridesmaids' gowns were punk. The whole color scheme of the decorations was punk.

— West Virginia *Mountaineer*

Wonder How Long His Horns Are?

A cattleman all his life, J. D. knows his breeds, and is noted for having the longest horns in all Texas.

— Paloma (Tex.) *Chieftain*

*　*　*

The Cats Were Probably Interested

For Sale: Farms and Mouses.

— Anthony (Kans.) *Republican*

*　*　*

Bet It's a Tight Fit

Mrs. M. D., who conducts the Aquin Book Shop, recently moved from Emmetsburg, Maryland, to Post Office Box 454, Cranford, New Jersey.

— *Booksellers' Magazine*

*　*　*

Gosh! Wonder How Old Mother Is?

Edward K. was guest of honor at a surprise birthday party recently, the occasion of his 166th anniversary. The party was arranged by Edward's mother.

— Ocean City (Cal.) *Sentinel*

*　*　*

Maybe They Are; But Why Admit It?

We invite you to come in and see the new goons on the second floor of our department store.

— Claremore (Okla.)

Now, Boys!

More than 1,330 4-H boys and girls modeled dresses.

— Chicago Daily News

* * *

Got Any in Your School?

Mr. N. visited the schoolroom yesterday and lectured on "Destructive Pests." A large number were present.

— Grand Rapids (Mich.) Press

* * *

Smart Germ

Letter from Germ sent *New Era*

— Headline in Ordway (Colo.) New Era

* * *

Did the Squirrel Have a License?

A. K., Menard hunter, was released from Menard Hospital after treatment for a gunshot wound in the left leg. He was accidentally shot by another squirrel in a field near Murray.

— Murray (Pa.) News

* * *

Don't Say You Weren't Warned!

Watch out for the pancake supper sponsored by the Mikana Ladies' Aid.

— Rice Lake (Wis.) Chronotype

Of Course, Some Are Not So Lucky

Take out an accident insurance policy. One customer got her arm broken the other day and we paid her $500. You may be the lucky one tomorrow.

— Advertisement in Harlem (N.Y.) *News*

✳ ✳ ✳

Maybe His Playing Has Improved

H. G., who used to direct the Silver Cornet Band of this town, is applying to the state board for a pardon.

— Moline (Ill.) *Tribune*

MY COUNTRY 'TIS OF THEE

*The great men of our country are so doggone great
that sometimes it's hard to remember that
they liked to make a wisecrack
now and then, too.*

One day a burglar was arrested in the home of a
Washington society woman and the next night at a din-
ner party she was telling Supreme Court Justice Oliver
Wendell Holmes all about it.

"I went right down to the jail and talked to that burglar," she said. "I told him how evil his way of life was,
and how much happier he would be if he reformed. I
talked to him for two solid hours."

"Poor man," murmured Mr. Holmes. "Poor man!"

* * *

John Randolph and Henry Clay once had an argument
in the Senate. It was such an angry quarrel that they did
not speak to each other afterward for quite a while. One
day they met on Pennsylvania Avenue where the sidewalk was very narrow.

As Randolph came up, he looked Henry Clay in the
eye, and not moving an inch from the sidewalk, hissed,
"I never turn out for scoundrels!"

"I always do," said Mr. Clay as he stepped politely
off the walk and let Randolph pass.

Abraham Lincoln, when he was a lawyer instead of a President, often had to argue with a little lawyer who always boomed out in a loud voice about nothing in particular. He reminded Lincoln of a boat he'd once seen.

"Back in the days when I performed my part as a keel-boatman," said Lincoln, "I made the acquaintance of a trifling little steamboat which used to bustle and puff and wheeze about the Sangamon River. It had a five-foot boiler and seven-foot whistle, and every time it whistled, it stopped."

* * *

Here's Another Lincoln Story

"In the early days," said Lincoln, "a party of men went out hunting for wild boar. But the boar came upon them unawares, and they, scampering away, climbed trees, all save one, who, seizing the animal by the ears, undertook to hold him. After holding him for some time and finding his strength giving way, he cried out to his companions in the trees, 'Boys, come down and help me let go.'"

* * *

General Putnam, speaking to new recruits in the Revolutionary Army, wanted to make it plain that he wished to have only willing fighters.

"Now, boys," he said, "I don't wish to retain any of you who wish to leave, and therefore, if any one of you is dissatisfied and wishes to return to his home, he may signify the same by stepping six paces in front of the line.

"But," added General Putnam, "I'll shoot the first man who steps out."

* * *

When Benjamin Franklin was a child, it was the custom to say very long graces before meals. Benjamin got pretty tired of these long prayers, as any kid would.

One day the meat for the winter was being salted down in barrels, and Benjamin came up with this bright thought: "I think, Father, if you were to say grace over the whole cask once and for all, it would be a vast saving in time."

* * *

Professor Albert Einstein, who knew his algebra formulas, once gave what he thought was the best formula for success in life.

"If a is success in life, I should say the formula is a equals x plus y plus z, x being work and y being play."

"And what is z?" asked the newspaper reporter who was interviewing him.

"That," said Professor Einstein, "is keeping your mouth shut."

* * *

Calvin Coolidge probably did less talking than any other President of the United States. A Washington hostess once boasted she could make President Coolidge talk. One night at a dinner party she tried to make her boast good.

"Oh, Mr. President," she said, "I have just made a bet that I can make you say at least three words."

And Mr. Coolidge replied, "You lose."

* * *

Samuel F. B. Morse was a well-known painter before he invented telegraphy. He once painted a picture showing a man in the agonies of death, and asked a doctor friend of his to look at it.

"Well?" said Morse after the doctor had looked at it very, very carefully. "What's your opinion?"

The doctor straightened up and said firmly. "There's no doubt about it. Malaria!"

* * *

The great Daniel Webster was a guest at a dinner party, and the hostess was so overcome at entertaining the great man that she couldn't seem to let him alone long enough to enjoy himself. Instead, she kept saying that he was eating nothing at all, that the dinner probably did not please him, that he had no appetite.

Finally Daniel Webster got tired of all this chitter-chatter. So he turned to her and said with all his dignity, "Madam, permit me to assure you that I sometimes eat more than at other times, but never less."

Stories about our thirtieth President, Calvin Coolidge, abound. One has him finishing a meal in a dining car. The waiter comes up and asks, "Was your dinner all right, Mr. President?" President Coolidge looks up at him suspiciously and replies, "Was there anything wrong with it?"

* * *

Another Coolidge story has the President coming out of Sunday church services in his home town. Two reporters are waiting to question him.

FIRST REPORTER: "Been to church, Mr. President?"
THE PRESIDENT: "Yup."
SECOND REPORTER: "Enjoy the sermon, Mr. President?"
THE PRESIDENT: "Yup."
FIRST REPORTER: "What was the subject of the sermon?"
THE PRESIDENT: "Sin."
SECOND REPORTER: "And what did the preacher think about sin, sir?"
THE PRESIDENT: "He's agin it."

* * *

One More Mark Twain Story!

Mark Twain once said, "When I was a boy of 14, my father was so ignorant I could hardly stand to have the old man around. But when I got to be 21, I was astonished at how much the old man had learned in seven years."

When Mark Twain went to borrow a book from a neighbor's library, the owner said he would be glad to lend it to him, but he had made a rule that any book in his library must be used right there, and could not be taken away.

The next week the neighbor asked to borrow Mark Twain's lawn mower.

"Take it, and welcome," said Mark Twain happily. "Only under a recently adopted policy it is not to be used away from my own lawn."

* * *

Mark Twain once sat listening to some tall stories friends of his were telling. At last Mark Twain could stand it no longer.

"Boys," he said, "these feats of yours that you've been telling about recall an adventure of my own in Hannibal. There was a fire in Hannibal one night, and old man Hankinson got caught in the fourth story of the burning house. It looked as if he was a goner. None of the ladders was long enough to reach him. The crowd stared at one another. Nobody could think of anything to do.

"Then all of a sudden, an idea occurred to me. 'Fetch a rope!' I yelled.

"Somebody fetched a rope, and with great presence of mind I flung the end of it up to the old man.

" 'Tie her round your waist!' I yelled.

"Old man Hankinson did so, and I pulled him down."

JOKES FOR THE FOLKS

*One of the best places to learn to tell jokes well is
right at home with your own folks. Here
are some to practice with, since most
folks like them.*

Mr. and Mrs. Parr were playing golf. As he drove off
the fourth tee, Mr. Parr sliced badly, and the ball hit
a woman who was also out golfing with her husband.

The husband, very angry, walked over to Mr. Parr.
"Why don't you watch what you're doing?" he asked.
"You hit my wife."

"Sorry, old man," said Mr. Parr. "Here's a ball. Take
a shot at mine."

* * *

Two ants were running like the wind across a cracker
box.

"Say, for Pete's sake," puffed one of them at last,
"what are we running so fast for?"

"Can't you read?" asked the other ant. "It says right
here 'Tear along the dotted line.'"

* * *

WIFE: "Well, what happened when you asked your
boss for a raise today?"

HUSBAND: "Why, he was like a lamb."

WIFE: "What did he say?"

HUSBAND: "Baa."

"Man overboard!" shouted the young sailor on his first voyage.

The ship was stopped at once, and the captain got ready to bring her around and try to find the drowning passenger.

The young sailor hurried to the bridge and saluted. "I'm sorry, sir, I made a mistake when I said 'Man overboard!'"

"Thank goodness!" said the captain, and signaled for full steam ahead.

"Yeah," said the young sailor. "It was a dame."

* * *

Two hunters had been in the woods for many hours, and there was no getting around the fact that they were lost.

"What shall we do?" cried one, in a panic. "We are lost!"

"Don't get so excited," said his friend. "Shoot an extra deer. The game warden'll find us inside of thirty seconds."

* * *

BUTCHER: "I'm sorry, but we have no ducks today. How about a nice leg of lamb?"

HUNTER: "Don't be silly. I can't tell my wife I shot a leg of lamb, can I?"

* * *

The preacher came along and wrote on a handy blackboard: I PRAY FOR ALL.

A lawyer came along and wrote under that: I PLEAD
FOR ALL.

The doctor wrote: I PRESCRIBE FOR ALL.

A plain citizen (your dad, probably) read these carefully and thought a while. Then he wrote: I PAY FOR ALL.

* * *

"Don't let me miss my train," said the boring visitor
to his host, who was driving him to the station.

"Don't worry," said his host. "My wife'll kill me if I
do."

* * *

OLD GENT: "I feel like a two-year-old today."
YOUNG GENT: "Horse, child, or egg?"

* * *

SAINT PETER: "How'd you get up here?"
NEW ARRIVAL: "Flu."

* * *

TEACHER: "Come, now. Define capital for us."
STUDENT, after thinking it over: "Well, capital's the
money the other fellow has."
TEACHER: "Good! Now what's labor?"
STUDENT, brightly: "Trying to get any of it away from
him."

An old couple went to the zoo and saw two kangaroos. One of the keepers strolled over.

"They are natives of Australia, you know," explained the keeper.

"You don't say!" gasped the old lady. "And to think that my poor sister married one of them."

✣   ✣   ✣

Boss: "How come you're only carrying one sack, when the other men are carrying two?"

Workman: "Well, I suppose they're too lazy to make two trips, the way I do."

✣   ✣   ✣

Waiter: "Do you want the dollar steak or the dollar and a quarter steak, sir?"

Sir: "What's the difference?"

Waiter: "You get a sharp knife with the dollar and a quarter steak."

✣   ✣   ✣

The fond mother beamed, "My daughter has arranged a little piece for the piano."

Not-so-fond neighbor: "Good! it's about time we had a little peace."

✣   ✣   ✣

Customer: "I haven't come to any ham in this ham sandwich yet."

Waitress: "Try another bite."

CUSTOMER, after taking a large bite: "No, none yet."

WAITRESS: "Doggone it! You must have gone right past it."

* * *

DUMB: "What're you doing?"

DUMBER: "Writing a letter to my little brother."

DUMB: "G'wan. You don't know how to write."

DUMBER: "That's O.K. My little brother doesn't know how to read."

* * *

SOPH: "Good heavens, get me a shovel quick! George is stuck in the mud up to his shoelaces!"

SENIOR: "His shoelaces! Why doesn't he just walk out, then?"

SOPH: "Stop arguing. He went in head first."

* * *

EDITOR: "Did you write this poem yourself?"

POET: "Every line of it."

EDITOR: "Then I'm very pleased to meet you, Edgar Allan Poe. I thought you were dead."

* * *

"The very idea!" said Mrs. Simpson. "The grocer cheated me on my order." So she telephoned the grocer angrily.

"What's the idea of short-weighting a little boy? I sent Johnny down to your store to get me three pounds of marshmallows. He just got home, and the bag of marsh-mallows weighs exactly one pound."

"I can't understand it," said the puzzled grocer. "I have my scales checked regularly. They give honest weight, and so do I."

The grocer thought a bit, and then asked, "Say, have you tried weighing Johnny?"

*　*　*

"Waiter," said the irritated customer, "I don't like all these flies that are buzzing around my dinner."

"Yes, sir," said the eager waiter. "You just point out to me the ones you don't like and I'll chase them away."

*　*　*

Mrs.: "What are you stopping the car for?"

Mr.: "The map from the auto club says to turn north and follow the trolley. We'll have to wait for a trolley to come along."

*　*　*

Mama: "George, you should speak to Junior about swearing. I overheard him using terrible language on the way home from school this afternoon."

Papa: "What! Swearing! I'll teach him to swear."

So Papa starts up the stairs, and on the top step stumbles over Junior's skates.

Mama, after Papa rolls to a stop and pauses for breath: "That's enough for one lesson, George."

Antique Collector: "Come, come. How could both Napoleon and George Washington have slept in this one bed?"

Antique Dealer: "Notice that this is a double bed."

* * *

"So you like my dog," said Mr. New Rich. "I'm glad. It's a very rare breed. Part boxer and part bull. It cost me a thousand dollars."

"Indeed?" said Mr. Ever Rich. "Which part is the bull?"

"The part about the thousand dollars," confessed Mr. New Rich.

* * *

"Guilty!" said the judge. "I'll give you ten days or twenty dollars."

"I'll take the twenty dollars, Judge," said the prisoner.

* * *

Father: "My boy, I never kissed a girl until I met your mother. Will you be able to say the same thing to your son?"

Junior: "Yes, Dad. But not with such a straight face."

* * *

"You told me that I'd get a good rest here because you didn't have any mosquitoes," complained the tired businessman after a night of slapping.

"I haven't," insisted the farmer who took summer boarders. "Those you've been slapping came over from next door. They're not mine."

* * *

The medicine show man was bragging about his wonderful herb tonic.

"Yes, gentlemen," he said, "I have sold this tonic for more than twenty-five years and never heard a word of complaint about it. Now, what does that mean?"

SMART KID: "That dead men tell no tales."

* * *

TRAMP: "Beg pardon, but do you happen to have some pie or cake that you could spare an unfortunate wanderer?"

LADY OF THE HOUSE: "No, I'm afraid not. Wouldn't some bread and butter do?"

TRAMP: "As a general rule, it would, but you see, today's my birthday."

* * *

"I don't like to criticize," said the English visitor, "but I do think our way of answering the telephone is better than yours."

PATRIOT: "Yeah! What do you say that's so much better?"

ENGLISH VISITOR: "Well, instead of saying 'Hello,' we say, 'Are you there?' Then, of course, if you're not there, there's no use going on with the conversation."

A motorist noticed that a farmer was having trouble
with his horse. It would start, go slowly for a while, and
then stop again. Then the farmer would have great
trouble getting the horse started once more. Finally the
motorist stopped and asked, "Is your horse sick?"

"No," said the disgusted farmer. "He's not sick."

"Is he balky?" asked the motorist.

"Nope, he's not balky."

"Then what's the matter with him?" asked the motorist.

"Well, stranger," said the disgusted farmer, "he's so
afraid I'll say whoa and he won't hear me that he stops
every once in a while to listen."

A young lady went into a drugstore and asked if it were possible to hide the taste of castor oil.

"It's horrid stuff, you know. Ugh!" And she shuddered at the thought of it.

"Why, certainly," said the druggist.

Just then another young lady sat down and ordered a chocolate ice cream soda. The druggist asked the patient if she wouldn't like one too. With a smile, she accepted, and drank the soda with much enjoyment.

"Now, tell me," she said. "How would you disguise the taste of castor oil?"

The druggist beamed all over. "Aha, my dear young lady, I just gave you some in that soda."

"But, good heavens!" screamed the young lady. "I wanted it for my sister."

❋ ❋ ❋

"Daddy," said the little boy, "how do wars start, anyhow?"

"Well, son," Dad started to explain, "let's say that America quarreled with England — "

"America is not quarreling with England," interrupted Mom.

"Who said she was?" Dad demanded. "I was just giving Junior an example."

"Ridiculous," snorted Mom. "You'll put all sorts of silly ideas into Junior's head."

"Ridiculous, nothing!" said Dad. "If he listens to you, he'll never have any ideas to put in his head."

Just as Mom picked up a dish and Dad dodged behind

a chair, Junior spoke up. "Thanks, Mom. Thanks, Dad. Boy, now I know exactly how wars start."

* * *

Young John Jones got home for the college holidays quite late. In fact, it was almost two o'clock in the morning. But John Jones couldn't wait to talk to his girl. So he called her up, and got the wrong number.

"Gosh, I'm sorry," apologized John Jones. "I'm terribly sorry for disturbing you."

"Oh, that's all right," said the sleepy wrong number. "You didn't disturb me. I had to get up to answer this confounded telephone, anyway."

* * *

Two old fishermen got into an argument one day about arithmetic, and each one was sure he knew more about arithmetic than the other. The argument got so hot that the captain of the fishing boat decided to take a hand in it, and he gave them a problem to work out. This was the test problem:

If a fishing crew caught 500 pounds of cod and brought their catch to port and sold it for 8 cents a pound, how much would they get for the fish?

The two fishermen went to work, but neither one of them seemed to get anywhere with the problem.

At last old Bill turned to the captain and asked him to repeat the problem. The captain agreed. "If a fishing crew caught 500 pound of cod — "

"Did you say they caught cod?" asked Bill.

"Sure," said the captain.

"Well, gol' dang it! No wonder I couldn't get the answer," said Bill. "Here I've been figuring on salmon all the time."

* * *

"Sam, wake up!"

"Mumff . . . Wassa matter?"

"Sam, I'm sure I heard a mouse squeak."

"Well, for Pete's sake. Whadda you want me to do? Get up and oil it?"

* * *

TEACHER, to student who is half an hour late to school: "You should have been here at nine o'clock."

STUDENT: "Why? What happened?"

* * *

On a bus the other day a man got up and gave a seat to a woman. She fainted.

When she came to, she thanked him. Then he fainted.

* * *

The newspaper editor was raking the new reporter over the coals. The reporter, it seemed, had turned in a story full of facts that weren't facts.

"In this business," finished the editor, "we don't say a thing is so unless we're sure it's so. Instead, we use such words as 'claimed,' 'reputed,' 'alleged,' 'rumored,' and so on. It keeps the paper out of trouble and lawsuits."

The young reporter took this lecture very much to heart. When he was sent out to report some of the social doings of the town, he sent in the following society item:

"It is rumored that a bridge party was given yesterday by a number of reputed ladies. Mrs. Smith, it is said, was hostess. The guests, it is alleged, with the exception of Mrs. Brown, who says she comes from Indiana, were all local people. Mrs. Smith claims to be the wife of Adam Smith, who is rumored to be doing a fine business in stocks and bonds."

* * *

Bill Brown was walking down the street one summer evening when he heard loud cries for help. A big man was beating a much smaller man.

"Here, you!" shouted Bill Brown. "Leave him alone." And Bill jumped into the fight, and pasted the big fellow on the chin.

"Thanks," said the little man after he had pulled himself together. "That was darned decent of you. Look here, you share this twenty bucks I took from him."

* * *

Little Georgie and his parents were making a trip across the ocean. The sea was rough, and Mama and Papa were very, very seasick. Little Georgie, unfortunately, enjoyed the best of health. He was a terrific nuisance to all the other passengers on board, and Mama, sick though she was, knew something would have to be done about little Georgie.

Finally, she said weakly, "Papa — I — wish — you'd — speak — to — Georgie."

Papa turned a sea-green face toward the badly behaving youngster. "How do you do, Georgie."

A canny young fisher named Fisher
Once fished from the edge of a fissure.
A fish with a grin
Pulled the fisherman in
Now they're fishing the fissure for Fisher.

TEACHER'S DAILY REPORT OF ABSENCE AND TARDINESS

Teacher		Class or Grade	Month	Day

MORNING			AFTERNOON	
NAME	AB-ABSENT T-TARDY		NAME	AB-ABSENT T-TARDY

19

FORM 320 SUPERIOR SCHOOL SUPPLIES, INC., PARSONS, KANSAS

PUNS

A pun is the lowest form of wit.
It does not tax the brain a bit.
You simply take a word that's plain
And pick one out that sounds the same.
Perhaps some letter may be changed
Or others slightly rearranged.
This to the meaning gives a twist
Which much delights the humorist.
A sample now may help to show
The way a good pun ought to go —

"It isn't the cough that carries you off. It's the coffin they carry you off in."
Get the idea?

* * *

SOPHOMORE: "What did you do last summer?"
SOPH: "I worked in Des Moines."
SOPHOMORE: "Iron or coal?"

* * *

HOPEFUL: "I see in the newspaper that a guy ate six dozen pancakes."
HOPELESS: "How waffle!"

SHIPWRECKED GAL: "Oh, oh! Cannibals!"

SHIPWRECKED PAL: "Come, now. Don't get into a stew."

* * *

DRIP: "See that dog chasing his tail."

DOPE: "Poor little cuss! He's trying to make both ends meet."

* * *

DRUGGIST: "Why is Dr. Williams so angry and snappy all the time?"

NURSE: "Oh, he's out of patients."

* * *

A little girl opened the door of the new refrigerator and found a very small squirrel curled up comfortably on the lower shelf.

"What are you doing there?" asked the little girl.

"Isn't this refrigerator a Westinghouse?" asked the very small squirrel.

"Yes, it is."

"Well," said the very small squirrel, "Ise westing."

* * *

This teacher wanted to be sure her pupils could use new words, too. So she said, "Now, boys and girls, we have been studying about the famous Prince Machiavelli. Can anybody use his name in a sentence?"

So the tailor's little boy jumped to his feet.

"My father," he said, "can Machiavelli fine sport coat for around twenty dollars."

The rain came down in torrents, faster and faster, harder and harder.

"It's raining cats and dogs," sighed the girl.

"I know," said the boy. "I just stepped in a poodle."

WORSE VERSE

Why in the world can everybody learn poems like these, but can't remember more than two lines of "Ode to a Grecian Urn"?

The gum-chewing girl
And the cud-chewing cow
Are somewhat alike
Yet different somehow.
And what is the difference?
I think I know now —
It's the clear, thoughtful look
On the face of the cow!

* * *

I wish I were a kangaroo
Despite his funny stances.
I'd have a place to put the junk
My girl brings to the dances.

I've never seen a purple cow.
I never hope to see one.
But just the same I'd rather see
A purple cow than be one.
— Gellett Burgess

FLEAS*

Adam
Had 'em.

*It won't do any good at all to read this one
unless you've studied chemistry:*

Alas for Little Willie!
We'll not see Willie more.
For what he thought was H_2O
Was H_2SO_4.

* * *

Women's faults are many.
Men have only two:
Everything they say,
And everything they do.

* * *

THE MONKEY'S WEDDING

The monkey married the baboon's sister,
Smacked his lips and then he kissed her,
Kissed her so hard that he raised a blister.
She set up a yell.
The bridesmaid stuck on some court plaster.
It stuck so fast it couldn't stick faster.
Surely it was a sad disaster,
But it soon got well.

* Believed by many English teachers to be the shortest poem ever written.

What do you think the bride was dressed in?
White gauze veil and the green glass breast pin,
Red kid shoes — quite interesting —
She was quite a belle.
The bridegroom swelled with a blue shirt collar,
Black silk stock that cost a dollar,
Long false whiskers, the mode to follow.
He cut a monstrous swell.

What do you think they had for supper?
Black-eyed peas and bread and butter,
Ducks in the duck-house all in a flutter,
Pickled oysters, too.
Chestnuts raw and boiled and roasted,
Apples sliced and onions toasted,
Music in the corner posted,
Waiting for the cue.

What do you think was the tune they danced to?
"The Drunken Sailor" — and sometimes "Jim Crow."
Tails in the way — and some got pinched, too,
'Cause they were too long.

What do you think they had for a fiddle?
And old banjo with a hole in the middle,
A tambourine made out of a riddle,
And that's the end of my song.

A pair in a hammock
Attempted to kiss
And in less than a jiffy
They landed like this.

* * *

SING A SONG OF CITIES

Said little Johnnie to the Owl,
"I've heard you're wondrous wise,
And so I'd like to question you;
Don't tell me any lies.

"The first thing, then, I'd have you tell
My empty mind to fill,
Say, was it the O'Leary cow
That made Chicago, Ill.?

"I've heard it said, yet do not know —
In fact, it may be bosh —
But tell me, is it lots of dirt
That makes Seattle, Wash.?

"This is the time of running debts,
As you must surely know.
This question, then, I'd like to ask:
How much does Cleveland, O.?

"In ages, too, you must be wise,
More so than many men.
So tell me in a whisper, please,
When was Miss Nashville, Tenn.?

"It takes great heat the gold to melt,
And iron takes much more;
Then is it true that way out West
The rain melts Portland, Ore.?

"Some voices are so strong and full,
And some so still and small,
That I have wondered oftentimes
How loud could Denver, Col.?"

The Owl scratched his feathered head.
"I'm sorry, little man.
Ask someone else. I cannot tell.
Perhaps Topeka, Kan."

❀   ❀   ❀

O, MLE, what XTC
I always feel when UIC.
I used to rave of LN's eyes,
For LC I gave countless sighs,
4 KT, 2, and LNR,
I was a keen competitor.
But each now's a non-NTT,
4 U XL them all, UC.

FATHER WILLIAM

"You are old, Father William," the young man said,
"And your nose has a look of surprise;
Your eyes have turned round to the back of your head,
And you live upon cucumber pies."
"I know it, I know it," the old man replied,
"And it comes from employing a quack,
Who said if I laughed when the crocodile died, I should
      never have pains in my back."

"You are old, Father William," the young man said,
"And your hair has become very white;
And yet you incessantly stand on your head —
Do you think, at your age, it is right?"
"In my youth," Father William replied to his son,
"I feared it might injure the brain!
But now that I'm perfectly sure I have none,
Why, I do it again and again."

"You are old, Father William," the young man said,
"And your legs always get in your way;
You use too much mortar in mixing your bread,
And you try to drink timothy hay."
"Very true, very true," said the wretched old man,
"Every word that you tell me is true;
And it's caused by my having my kerosene can
Painted red where it ought to be blue."

                      — Lewis Carroll

He went out one lovely night
To call upon a miss.
And when he reached her residence,
                                    this.
                        like
                stairs
            up
        ran
He
Her father met him at the door.
He didn't see the miss
And he'll not visit there again, for
He
        went
            down
                stairs
                    like
                        this.

* * *

THE WHITING AND THE SNAIL

"Will you walk a little faster?" said a whiting to a snail,
"There's a porpoise close behind us, and he's treading
    on my tail.
See how eagerly the lobsters and the turtles all advance.
They are waiting on the shingle. Will you come and join
    the dance?
Will you, won't you, will you, won't you, will you join
    the dance?
Will you, won't you, will you, won't you, won't you join
    the dance?

"You can really have no notion how delightful it will be
When they take us up and throw us, with the lobsters,
    out to sea!"
But the snail replied, "Too far, too far!" and gave a look
    askance.
Said he thanked the whiting kindly, but he would not
    join the dance.
Would not, could not, would not, could not, would not
    join the dance;
Would not, could not, would not, could not, could not
    join the dance.

"What matters it how far we go?" his scaly friend replied.
"There is another shore, you know, upon the other side.
The farther off from England, the nearer is to France.
Then turn not pale, beloved snail, but come and join
    the dance.
Will you, won't you, will you, won't you, will you join
    the dance?
Will you, won't you, will you, won't you, won't you join
    the dance?"

— Lewis Carroll

*　*　*

'Twas in a restaurant they met,
Romeo and Juliet.
He had no cash to pay the debt,
So Romeo'd what Juli-et.

The centipede was happy quite
Until a toad in fun
Said, "Pray, which leg comes after which?"
This raised her mind to such a pitch
She lay distracted in a ditch
Wondering how to run.